CW00570986

SHORTS - THE FOREMAN YEARS

Guy Warren

March 2008.

First Published in 2008 by The Ulster Aviation Society, Belfast

ISBN 978 1 905989 93 5

All photographs by kind permission of Bombardier, Belfast, unless otherwise stated

This book has been printed on elemental chlorine free paper, which is fully recyclable and biodegradable.

Design: D4 Design
Printing: Nicholson & Bass Ltd

Sir Philip Foreman at his desk at Shorts in Belfast

CONTENTS

FOREWORD – THE ULSTER AVIATION SOCIETY

Founded 1968

Ulster has an aviation history which bears a very favourable comparison with other regions of Great Britain and Ireland. There are many aspects to it, including the development of civil flying and commercial air services, this country's vital contribution to defending the United Kingdom during two world wars and aircraft manufacturing, to name but four. Human beings being the life blood of history, one thinks of historical personalities of Ulster birth or adoption who have made contributions of particular significance including Harry Ferguson, Sir James Martin and the 7th Marquis of Londonderry for example.

Awareness of that history and the important role that aircraft production has played in the country's socio-economic development has, I believe, inspired the foundation, growth and continuing development of the Ulster Aviation Society. This voluntary association of aviation enthusiasts was inaugurated in 1968 and currently has a membership of around 250. In 1997, the Society was re-constituted, on the basis of which it was recognised as a charity by Her Majesty's Inland Revenue, reflecting primary aims which are fundamentally educational in nature.

Even before 1997 and since, the Society has been responsible for or associated with numerous publications of which this book is the latest. It is a book for which I feel specially privileged to have been asked to write a foreword, for a number of reasons. Firstly, it is being published during the 40th year of the Society's existence and I regard it as one manifestation of our celebration of this notable anniversary.

What is of more importance however is that the subject of the book, Sir Philip Foreman, CBE, DL, FR Eng, FIAE, as Patron, is a much respected source of inspiration and encouragement to Society members by virtue of his illustrious and uniquely important contribution to the sustained development of the aerospace industry of Northern Ireland. He fulfils the role of Patron superbly well, bringing to it many of the qualities, and more, he demonstrated so effectively during his aviation career, generously supporting and maintaining a close interest in the Society's affairs while respecting the voluntary management ethos of the association.

In the following pages, my Society colleague Guy Warner lists and reflects on many of those qualities and I am pleased he has included a reference to Sir Philip's perseverance, which must have been tested to near breaking point at the worst of times during "the Troubles". To his great credit, however, he remained loyal to Shorts during the worsening political climate of the 'seventies which drove men of lesser fibre from all walks of life to up stakes and leave the country altogether. To Guy's list, moreover, I would add faith in and affection for the Ulster people, no better demonstration of which can be found than in Sir Philip and Lady Foreman's decision to continue living in Northern Ireland in retirement. Notwithstanding his status, he and Margaret are a most friendly and engaging couple and those of us who value the best interests of our community as well as our aviation heritage owe them an immense debt of gratitude.

Ernie Cromie,
Chairman Ulster Aviation Society

FOREWORD – THE NORTHERN IRELAND INDUSTRIAL BACKGROUND

When the future Sir Philip Foreman came to Belfast in 1958, it was a big decision for a young engineer of 35. He had a secure civil service job with the Admiralty. In contrast, Shorts was a company whose unusual financial relationship with the Government of the day introduced an element of uncertainty into its future. But he was attracted by the potential of the guided weapons division when the dynamic Hugh Conway, the Canadian-born, Scottish and English-educated managing director, asked him to join the team, with full responsibility for design and development of all the equipment associated with the Seacat project. Within nine years, Foreman had stepped into Conway's shoes as managing director.

The Northern Ireland of 1967 was very much another country and would feel entirely strange to the younger generation today. Terence O'Neill had been elected leader of the governing Unionist Party only four years before. But it was much less than a total vote of confidence in the ex-Irish Guardsman from Ahoghill in Co Antrim. The party was split because, while O'Neill appealed to the traditionalists, many of them old-fashioned liberals warming to the leadership of a scion of one of the ancient families, Brian Faulkner of the shirt manufacturing family, of Seaforde, Co Down was a sharper individual altogether, appealing to his peers in the business class, who were convinced that he was by far the abler candidate. Possibly it was the gentry's outmoded jealousy of "trade" which fired the lobby which kept him out.

But Faulkner accepted the key Commerce Ministry in O'Neill's Cabinet—and made a remarkable success of it. In the summer of 1966, unemployment in the province—unprecedentedly—sank below five per cent. Faulkner used his business expertise, most notably in London and New York, to attract more big names in the developing chemical industry, concentrating particularly on man-made fibres—which occupied the place in the industrial spectrum of the 1960s which advanced electronics do now. Within a space of a few years, Northern Ireland, with less than three per cent. of the United Kingdom's population, was producing 33 per cent of its synthetic fibre output, involving not only British manufacturers, but Dutch, German and American as well.

Alongside this innovation, the old bastions of Northern Ireland industry, although beginning to feel the chill of Asian competition, were still substantial operators. Davidson's Sirocco Works in east Belfast were still exporting their huge ventilation fans worldwide, not to mention its sizeable chunk of the world market in tea-drying machinery. Although Harland & Wolff had not made a profit for three years, it was heavily involved in equipping itself to compete in the new age of the supertanker and its future had not yet been called seriously into question. At James Mackie's foundry in west Belfast there was still a labour force of more than 6,000 in the 1960s, having added machinery for processing synthetic fibres to its traditional jute spinning frames.

But it was very much the calm before the storm. Politics thenceforward were to spill over violently to affect the commercial sphere; and for Shorts, there were domestic financial difficulties. In the months before Foreman took over as managing director, the company had been climbing out of the trough of despair into which it had been plunged by the Labour Government's bid to close it down. Now, although having fought its way to a reprieve, the company still had its back to the wall: for Whitehall actively intervened with overseas manufacturers who already had placed substantial work with Shorts, among them Fokker of the Netherlands and VFW of Germany, to prevent their placing further aviation contracts in Belfast.

The co-operation with the Germans was going so well that VFW now wanted the Belfast company to be partner in the launch of a small airliner. Soon it emerged that Whitehall had snuffed out this bid and had similarly told McDonnell Douglas that Shorts would not be permitted to do work on the American Phantom II fighter. Lockheed was told the same when it proposed to place work on its big C130 transport in Belfast. These disclosures, involving a full-scale boardroom row with the Government which culminated in mass resignations, had come to the boil just before Foreman took over the reins.

In the light of this history, Shorts' future successes under its own steam are thrown into formidable relief. When Foreman took over, the company—barred, unlike its competitors, from raising development capital in the financial markets—had accumulated debts of some £12m. (This may seem a modest burden today; but bear in mind that in 1967 the average houseowner's monthly mortgage repayment was only about £9 and his wife's weekly food bill a mere £7.) For Shorts, the ultimate test was to come when the Canadian Bombardier transport group was waiting in the wings in 1989 to buy it from the Government. That there was a vigorous, saleable entity surviving was a tribute to the team and to Sir Philip Foreman's leadership of it.

Eric Waugh

INTRODUCTION

It can be contended that the most sustained period of success for Shorts in its history was between the 1960s and 1980s. It is no coincidence that during those years Philip Foreman (now Sir Philip) held a succession of increasingly senior positions within the company. On his retirement in 1988 he did not let the grass grow beneath his feet, undertaking a number of consulting and non-executive appointments with the British Standards Institution, the Teaching Company, the Ricardo Group, Simon Engineering, Shurlock International SA and as Chairman of the Progressive Building Society (Belfast). He was awarded the CBE in 1972 for services to industry and export and was knighted in 1981. In 1974 he was awarded the British Empire Gold Medal by the Royal Aeronautical Society. He is an Honorary Doctor of Science at Queen's University, Belfast, Honorary Doctor of Technology at Loughborough University and an Honorary Doctor of the Open University. He is a fellow of both the Royal Academy of Engineering (FREng) and the Irish Academy of Engineering (IAE). He is also an Honorary Fellow of the Royal Aeronautical Society. He was formerly a Deputy Lieutenant of the City of Belfast, is a Freeman of the City of London and a Liveryman of the Worshipful Company of Engineers. Since 2003 he has been the Patron of the Ulster Aviation Society and has taken a great interest in the work of the Society.

Recently I had the pleasure of spending a number of hours talking to Sir Philip and his wife, Margaret, as they reminisced over his career in the aerospace industry in Northern Ireland. Many thanks are due to both of them for their time and hospitality. Grateful thanks are also due to the renowned journalist and political commentator, Eric Waugh, for his foreword on the Northern Ireland industrial scene in the 1960s, Malcolm Wild for organising my meeting with the Shorts "old hands", Alan McKnight, Ken Best and Paul McMaster for their tremendous help with the photographs, thanks also to John Nicholson, Don Hawthorn and Gary Shivers for the design and production of this book, Ernie Cromie for his foreword on the Ulster Aviation Society and his invaluable and meticulous proof reading and, as ever, to my very supportive and tolerant wife, Lynda.

Guy Warner
Carrickfergus
January 2008

EARLY YEARS

Philip Foreman's earliest memories are of learning the "three Rs" from his mother, Mary, before and during his early schooldays at Exning Church of England Elementary School. His was a happy home and, as an only child, he was the apple of his mother's eye, who was a quietly supportive, formative influence. Aviation was not the inspiration for the young Philip on the Cambridgeshire farm where he grew up in the 1920s and 1930s. He was much more interested in Meccano, model steam engines and the agricultural machinery which his father, Frank, drove, maintained and repaired – although he did cycle some 10 miles to Mildenhall to see the start of the MacRobertson England to Australia air race on October 20, 1934 when he was eleven years old. It was about this time also that he won a scholarship to Soham Grammar School, where one of his contemporaries was John WR Taylor, who would later become a well-respected aviation author.

Philip displayed considerable sporting prowess at school. A contemporary, Wilkes Walton recalls, "Phil was a sturdy lad and pretty quick, who took some stopping on the rugby field. I also played with Phil in the Cricket XI in 1941 - my first season and Phil's last year at school. The *Soham Grammarian* noted in the Summer 1941 issue, "At this point it is fitting that we congratulate our popular Head Boy, PF Foreman, on his magnificent achievement. He has won a British Empire Open Scholarship of the value of £75 a year tenable for three years at

Philip with his mother and father
(FOREMAN FAMILY COLLECTION)

Philip looking very serious in a school photograph taken in about 1937
(SOHAM GRAMMAR SCHOOL)

Loughborough College. Four others were awarded to pupils of secondary schools in the British Empire."

His mechanical bent was nurtured at Loughborough College, from where he graduated in 1943 with a First Class Honours Diploma in Mechanical Engineering. Looking back, Sir Philip greatly values the "good basic grounding" he received on a course which comprised academic study interspersed with workshop based training. He believes that it produced, "Good, honest, practical engineers who could relate academic work to the real world of engineering and commerce."

ADMIRALTY RESEARCH

Colour blindness having thwarted his desire to join the Royal Navy in 1941, on graduating from Loughborough, he was directed to the RN Scientific Service and so became a Temporary Experimental Assistant Grade 3, at the princely salary of £200 pa, at the Admiralty Research Establishment, Teddington, Middlesex.

Much of his early work there involved the development of remote control hydraulic servo-systems for naval guns and gunnery directors; this included the Bofors 40mm which was used to shoot down German V1 "Doodle Bugs". Later he

Skyraider approaching touchdown
(JIM COWELL)

Skyraider landing
(JIM COWELL)

worked on the stabilization of the Mirror Deck Landing System for aircraft carriers. This brought the never-to-be-forgotten experience of his first ever flight – from HMS *Daedalus*, Lee-on-Solent in a Douglas Skyraider to land on HMS *Illustrious* in the English Channel to take part in the sea trials of the system. Sir Philip recalls, "To this day I vividly remember my relief when the aircraft came to a shuddering halt on the deck as it caught the third arrestor wire. Down below in the Wardroom, a colleague remarked how strange it was that the lighting had turned my face green, he was assured that this was no trick of the light!"

By 1958 he was a Senior Scientific Officer. One of his major projects at that time was designing the launcher for the brand new Seacat missile system.

HMS Illustrious
(AUTHOR'S COLLECTION)

PRECISION ENGINEERING

The missile was a product of Shorts' Precision Engineering Division which had been founded at Castlereagh in 1952 and which had had some early success with the design and production of the first general purpose analogue computer - exhibited at Farnborough in 1953 and selling over the next few

Shorts Precision Engineering Division at Castlereagh

years some 72 of these in total at £5300 a time.

The Royal Navy was interested in a low-cost missile to replace the Bofors gun. Shorts began with the General Purpose Vehicle (GPV) which tested propulsion, guidance and control systems, telemetry and instrumentation. 40 GPVs were built from the time of its first launch in 1953. In 1956 Shorts gained the contract to research a short-range, anti-aircraft (AA) missile.

This was the Green Light Test Vehicle (GLTV) which was manually controlled and visually guided. The experience gained designing, building, testing and flight-testing the GPV and the GLTV gave Castlereagh the expertise to progress in the guided weapons field. Its selected niche was the close-range AA missile with a range of up to 6km to defend ships or a land-

Seacat components in production

based military installation. Work on the Seacat system – missile, launcher and director – also got under way in 1956. A production site was set up at Queen's Island and the first Seacat production contract for the RN was agreed in 1957. Shorts built the electronics, airframe, wings, control and guidance systems, as well as the test equipment. The fuse, motor and warhead were outsourced. The whole package was then assembled in Royal Naval Armament Depots.

Philip Foreman's work on the Seacat launcher had come to the notice of Shorts' Chief Engineer, Hugh Conway, who persuaded him to join the company and come to Belfast in October 1958 to look after the design and development of all the shipborne and armament depot equipment associated with Seacat. This was quite a challenge but the years at Teddington had been of great benefit, which Sir Philip later described as, "I met and worked with men of great engineering ability and in many respects my first five years were not unlike a vast post-graduate apprenticeship. I was fortunate in being involved in multi-disciplinary development work which instilled in me the system approach to engineering which has been so important throughout my career." Formative influences at Teddington included the Deputy Director JM Ford and the Head of Power Group TJ Tooley.

EARLY YEARS AT SHORTS

His first task for Shorts was to design the visual director from which the complete Seacat system was controlled. Seacat made its Farnborough debut in 1959. Development trials then took place at Aberporth in the same year. These were followed by sea trials on board HMS *Decoy* in 1961. It was accepted into service by the RN in 1962 and also won the Queen's Award to Industry for Technical Innovation – one of many Queen's Awards to be won by Shorts. By the late 1960s Seacat was in service with 13 countries and was the world's most widely sold guided weapon system.

The Seacat director and launcher on board HMS Decoy

Seacat visual director Sea Trials HMS Decoy

A Seacat is captured by the camera at the moment of launch from the HMAS Yarra

Martin Armour, Rex Galway, Jim Foye, Wally Galloway, Peter Hill, Reg Harriman, Dick Ransom, Fred Lowens, Billy Turner, Phil Foreman, David Kennedy and Seacat.

Seacat Quad launcher

Seacat missiles ready for dispatch

Philip Foreman greatly enjoyed his time at Castlereagh as part of a highly motivated and very able design team, which included Martin Armour, John Sendles, Dick Ransom, Rex Galway, Frank Maguiness, Wally Galloway and Jim Foye. It was a very friendly place at which to work – once the ice had been broken and Philip had proved his ability to his colleagues that he was more than just an English interloper. To a certain extent, Castlereagh was a law unto itself as the work was so different from aircraft building. Most of the team were quite young and were dynamic and progressive. Brainstorming sessions once a month on a Friday afternoon to solve problems were the norm as the goal was achieved more through multi-disciplinary teamwork rather then individual glory hunting. The contrast with working for the Admiralty was marked, "Within that service the overriding concern was technical excellence and the people concerned were indisputably of the highest scientific and technical calibre. In industry, on the other hand, I found a vastly greater appreciation of the need to design for production and a greater sense of urgency to get things done. But somewhat surprisingly, I also discovered a much higher incidence of internal meetings and a greater volume of paperwork to record the proceedings – not the other way round as might have been expected." By 1961 he had risen to the position of Chief Engineer of the Guided Weapons Division.

In 1964 he was attending the Farnborough Airshow when Hugh Conway, who was by that time the Joint Managing Director, asked Philip to accompany him back to London in his car, he said in fact, "How are you getting back to London? Get into the car and shut up." Mr Conway (as he was known) advised him that he was leaving Shorts for Bristol Siddeley and that he had recommended Philip to be Company Chief Engineer. This was quite a jump and a considerable challenge. Philip's immediate response was, "But I know nothing about aeroplanes." The reply was blunt and to the point, "You'll soon learn!" Having thought it over, he reflected with more excitement than trepidation, "Well I respect Mr Conway's opinion and if he thinks I can do it, then I must be able to." He regarded the Canadian-born Hugh Conway as an excellent leader, with a brilliant, innovative, constructive mind. Conway was a doer and was highly respected by all his staff. He was also ahead of his time in his approach to the media with whom he was also popular. The sign above his desk summed up his approach in a tongue in cheek fashion, "Don't bother me with facts, my mind is made up!" Philip also had a great deal of respect for the very shrewd and able, long-serving Chairman, Rear Admiral Sir Matthew Slattery, who had left the company in 1960 to become Chairman of BOAC.

COMPANY CHIEF ENGINEER

The first challenge was to gain the respect of the senior technical team at Queen's Island, all of whom had an aircraft engineering background and which included Denis Hatton, Frank Robertson, and Bob Boorman. With hindsight, Sir Philip now believes that it was actually an advantage to have come from a different engineering discipline, "Not being a traditional aeronautical engineer, I could apply the system approach I had learned in the Admiralty in an unemotional clinical manner." There was also some resistance from some old Shorts sweats from the Rochester days, with remarks such as, "How many people will those fireworks you make at Castlereagh carry?"

Hugh Conway

The Shorts SB5 research aircraft provided much valuable data for the English Electric Lightning supersonic fighter. It flew for the first time with wings swept back by 69 degrees at RAE Bedford In October 1960.

VC-10 Sub-contract work in 1964

The SC 1 hovers watched closely by the fire crews

From the post-war years to the 1960s, Shorts aircraft work could best be described as a very mixed bag – the last flying-boats, Sandringhams, Solents and Scalands; conversion work on the Handley Page Halton and Junkers JU-52/3M; one-off government contracts, the SA 4 Sperrin, SB 4 Sherpa, SB 5 and SC 1; two promising but ultimately unsuccessful naval types, the Sturgeon and the Seamew; other companies designs - complete aircraft - the Bristol Britannia and the English Electric Canberra (the PR 9 version of which was designed and built by Shorts) and sub-contracting on the DH Comet and Vickers VC-10.

Canberras on the production line at Queen's Island

The Shorts SC1 first achieved transition from jet-borne hovering to wing-borne flight and the reverse at RAE Bedford on April 6th, 1960

Belfast XR362 takes off from Sydenham

The biggest technical challenge facing the company at that time was the SC 5 Belfast freighter (until the advent of the C-17 Globemaster III over 30 years later it was the largest aircraft to see service with the RAF). Its maiden flight had been on January 5, 1964, when XR362 took off from Sydenham and crossed Belfast Lough to land at Aldergrove, flown by Short's chief test pilot, Denis Tayler with co-pilot Peter Lowe and a crew of six,. Developing the autoland capability (in partnership with Smiths) was a task of considerable complexity. It was the first military aircraft in service to incorporate the Smith Series Five Flight Control System, providing triplexed autoland capability, making it the largest aircraft in the world to make fully automatic landings – experienced by Philip Foreman on a flight to Schipol Airport, Amsterdam, with test pilot, Don Wright. He remembers watching the drips of sweat fall from Don's chin, as he monitored with intense concentration a perfect hands-off approach and landing. Further developments of the aircraft

were planned - for tactical operations from rough strips, with uprated engines and larger propellers to increase performance, a swing-nose, double-deck civil transport, a Skybolt missile platform or with a new wing and tail (adapted from the Lockheed C-141 Starlifter) and fitted with turbofan engines. As *Flight* magazine stated in 1963, "No company ever tried harder to perfect all aspects of a sound basic aeroplane than have Short & Harland with the Belfast. No company ever tried harder to develop it to meet every conceivable future requirement." But the orders never came and the support received from the government was less than ideal – the original contract was predicated on an order for 30 aircraft, which was then cut to only ten and nearly brought the company to ruin, as only a third of the non-recurring costs were now recoverable.

Confidence in an aircraft manufacturing future for Belfast was not enhanced by the publication of the UK Government's Plowden Report at the end of 1965, which recommended the

Belfast G-ASKE (later XR362 'Samson' then G-BEPE) makes its first appearance
October 8th, 1963

Belfast XR363 'Goliath at Sydenham 1964

amalgamation of Britain's aircraft manufacturers into two large companies – a place for Shorts within this scheme was not envisaged. The Minister of Aviation, Roy Jenkins, told Shorts, "You know that the Plowden Report isn't favourable towards you." which was something of an understatement. Nor was the company in any fit state to go it alone as a commercial manufacturer, since it had existed for years on a diet of military contracts. A report from a consultancy firm stated, "It has no commercial marketing organisation worthy of the name and a management group which is experienced almost exclusively in supplying the requirements of one customer. Performance and adherence to a particular schedule of deliveries is generally paramount. Price is a secondary consideration. Extensive and continuous formal documentation of production progress, engineering changes and justification of any changes in the cost is required by the military. The net result is the need for a high proportion of indirect workers of all kinds – technical, managerial and administrative – to direct labour; which could not be justified in a normal commercial business". At that time the company had a total payroll of some 7800 employees, of whom 6100 were employed on aircraft and related work, 1300 on precision engineering (including guided weapons) and the balance of 400 on general engineering. The annual turnover was in the region of £14 million.

MANAGING DIRECTOR

Only three years after becoming Chief Engineer, there was further promotion, this time to Managing Director (he had been appointed to the Board of Directors in 1965 and had become Deputy Managing Director in the following year). Now the destiny and direction of one of the most important parts of Northern Ireland's industrial base was Philip Foreman's responsibility, quite a remarkable rise after only nine years with the company. This was reported in the *Belfast Telegraph* on

Shorts Belfast site

January 3, 1967, which quoted the newly appointed MD as follows, "There is no reason why the company should not develop another aircraft along the same lines as the Skyvan. But I can't see us doing anything as big as the Belfast freighter again. It's just too large an aeroplane for us." When asked about Shorts future prospects he responded in typical style, "Certainly Shorts has a viable future. Do you think I would be here if it didn't?" adding, "It will be a long, hard grind and a lot of hard work but we are going to get through."

The problems which had to be faced were severe, "We had to make major decisions on where our future best lay, especially since the production of the Belfast was rapidly coming to an end. With a business based predominantly on the manufacture of military aircraft against Ministry of Defence orders, we clearly had to re-think our plans." One obvious option was to re-trench, cut back and concentrate on the growing and successful missiles business.

As well as developments improving the basic naval Seacat, which included transistors replacing thermionic valves and the production of the lightweight three round launcher; a land-based system had been introduced. The Commandant of RAF Regiment, Air Chief Marshal Sir Philip Joubert de la Ferte had seen the need for an airfield defence system and had pressed for the development of what would become Tigercat, the first firing of which was in 1967. It was tested by the RAF Regiment in a deployment around Sydenham. It was cheap, adaptable and comparatively simple, with a launcher and control console capable of being towed by Land Rover. It was to sell well. The Defence Sales Organisation, which was established by Denis Healey when he was Minister of Defence between 1964 and

RAF Tigercat deployed at Sydenham

Tigercat on the launcher

1970, worked closely with Shorts, providing information from Defence Attaches around the world, on the lines of, "There's a ship being built – perhaps you can sell Seacat there." But this would not be enough to keep in employment most of those who depended upon the company for their livelihood.

However it was decided not to go the missile-only route, which would have been a sad end to Shorts' proud history as an aircraft manufacturer. Instead Philip Foreman's policy after becoming MD was to make the missile business one facet of a tripartite structure, the other two components being a small civil transport aeroplane and aerostructures, the building blocks already being in place for both of these. He worked on the principle that a milking stool has three legs and is therefore very stable and what was a good enough rule for the farmer was equally applicable to Shorts. Another major decision was to close the general engineering division at Newtownards, introduced in the 1950s which had in its day ensured the survival of the company during a difficult decade by turning its hand to all sorts of manufacturing - aluminium frame buildings, which included schools and hospitals, fork-lift trucks, straddle carriers, dishwashers, oil filled radiators, milk churns, wringers and carpet sweepers – but which was by then commercially uncompetitive. The range of diversified activities was too broad. An insufficient foothold was held in a range of markets with products which were only marginally profitable and which were often over-designed for commercial success.

THE SKYVAN

The civil project was the SC 7 Skyvan, unkindly referred to by some as "a flying shoe-box with a ruler across the top" - the prototype of which, G-ASCN, had flown for the first time at 11.15am on January 17, 1963, in the hands of Denis Tayler. As the house magazine *Short Story* reported, "After a flight lasting only a few minutes, the portly shape scurried - or should it be

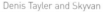

Denis Tayler and Skyvan

The Skyvan's maiden flight January 17th, 1963
(BELFAST NEWSLETTER)

trundled? - home pursued by a menacing snow cloud." A cartoon in the same issue depicted the aircraft as a removals van, complete with pilot clad in flat cap and overalls putting his feet up on an adjacent sofa. The Skyvan had a fixed undercarriage and was decidedly cuboid in shape. In its original piston-engine form it was underpowered and overweight. For a number of reasons, "not least internal discord over the project within the company – it was a technical disaster." Some

The Skyvan prototype on a snowy runway at Sydenham on 21st January 1963, a few days after its maiden flight

Still with piston engines, the Skyvan landing at Sydenham in February 1963

Skyvan Astazou prototype G-ASCN takes off from Sydenham in October 1963

The Skyvan G-ASCN over the Mournes in 1964

The Skyvan Prototype - taxiing trials at Sydenham 6th January 1963

Parachutists exiting Skyvan

progress was made by changing the engines to turbo-props, the first flight of which was on October 29, 1963 (G-ASCN again). The first customer deliveries were made in 1966; to Aeralpi, I-TORE, in June and to Emerald Airways, G-ATPF, in August. However the Turbomeca Astazou was dreadfully unreliable. It was particularly disappointing in hot and high conditions and also found considerable sales resistance in the USA, which was considered to offer the largest potential market for the Skyvan. The new MD was faced with the decision - should the project be abandoned or could it be salvaged? It was believed that if the engineering could be got right the aircraft could be a success as its large square fuselage was a highly marketable feature. The Board of Directors was divided and it took a majority decision to keep Skyvan alive by deciding to re-engine again, this time with the American Garrett AiResearch TPE331 turboprop. The majority shareholder, the Government, was not convinced and a meeting was held between the full Shorts Board and no less than five Government ministers, including Tony Benn and John Stonehouse, at which hard won approval to proceed was given. Within eight months and at some 20% less than budget the first

Garrett powered Skyvan Series 3, G-ASZI, flew for the first time on December 15, 1967 and immediately went into production. Sir Philip later commented, "I personally regard this particular decision and the subsequent success of Skyvan in the

Skyvan and tractor

Skyvan of the Royal Air Force of Oman

marketplace as a turning point in the shape of the company – or indeed maybe its very survival as an aircraft manufacturer. The project was taken into the mainstream of the company's activities, proper management and project control was instituted and it was given top level attention. It kept the company in the aircraft business at a time when we had no other complete aircraft project and no sensible plans for launching one."

The sales brochure described it thus, "When Shorts set out to build the Skyvan they did not just make an aeroplane and see how much could be fitted into it. They started the other way round. First, they built a big flying box. They made it easy to get things into this box by making the back end of the box into a door. Shorts made it strong and rugged. It will go almost anywhere, land on the most primitive airstrips and it's very easy to maintain. But the surprising thing about the Skyvan is its limitless versatility. It takes only minutes to convert from a 19-

passenger aircraft to a freighter carrying a load of 4600 lbs. It stands up to gruelling day and night operations without a murmur. Military uses include paratrooping, troop transport, supply dropping, vehicle ferry, counter-insurgency, clandestine warfare, casualty evacuation and civil disaster relief. Skyvan is not just a new aircraft. It's a new kind of aircraft. It's a bus, a train, a boat, a lorry, a car, a van - and it flies." Perhaps the most striking sales photograph was captioned, "An ox-cart off loads from the flying box-car at an equatorial jungle airstrip."

The largest Skyvan operator has been the Sultan of Oman's Air Force which acquired its first of an eventual fleet of 16 in May 1970. During 1983 extensive local modifications resulted in three aircraft being converted into Seavans for maritime operations. The prototype military Skyvan 3M, G-AXPT, first flew on March 30, 1969. This version featured weather radar in the nose radome, a port side blister window for an air

Skyvan G-ASZJ - which became the Skyliner prototype

dispatcher, accommodation for 16 paratroops or 22 soldiers or 12 stretcher cases or 5000lbs of freight. The first military operator of the Skyvan was the Austrian Air Force which acquired two aircraft in September 1969.

The Skyliner prototype, G-ASZJ, which was a 22 seat, all passenger version with an airstair-equipped entry door on the port side, flew for the first time in August 1970. Skyliners flew with several airlines including British European Airways (BEA).

A few years later Philip and Margaret Foreman made a very memorable visit to Washington to take part in a demonstration flight given to members of the US Civil Aeronautics Board (CAB) and their wives one Sunday morning in a specially equipped Skyvan, fitted with soft leather upholstered seats, as part of a lobbying campaign to have the 19 seat restriction

BEA Skyliner G-AZYW in flight

placed by the CAB on commuter aircraft raised to 30 seats, which was crucial to the further development and market penetration of the Skyvan and its successors. This was a somewhat more comfortable version than the pair operated by Northern Ireland's Emerald Airways in the 1960s – passengers were issued with ear plugs and rugs!

Never a glamorous aeroplane, the Skyvan was a post-war best seller for Shorts until surpassed by models developed from this basic but very practical concept. Production ceased in 1986 after the 153rd example, AGAW-121, which was delivered to the Amiri Guard Air Wing, Sharjah.

Skyliners for BEA on the production line

Belfast XR362 'Samson' dwarfs its sister aircraft the prototype Skyvan G-ASCN

AEROSTRUCTURES

The genesis of what was ultimately to become an extremely successful aerostructures division was the undertaking made in 1965 to design and develop the wings for the new Fokker F.28

Wings for the Fokker F.28

Aldergrove 1968, XT891, the first McDD Phantom for the RAF – outer wings by Shorts
(AUTHOR'S COLLECTION)

Fellowship short-range jet airliner. Another major sub-contract operation at this time was for the outer wings for the McDonnell Douglas Phantom.

The next stage in the development of this side of the business was recalled by Sir Philip as follows, "By good fortune, at this time (May 1968) Rolls-Royce was launching the RB211 engine and was looking for suppliers to design and manufacture the engine nacelle so that they could market a complete powerplant

RB211 nose cowl

instead of a bare engine. We managed to secure the contract for the nose cowl and for the final assembly of the complete nacelle around the engine. This work put us into a specialist niche where we could employ all our skills from aerodynamics through structures and systems to manufacture. By spotting and exploiting that market opportunity, we were able to become one of the world's leading manufacturers of nacelles for large turbo-fan engines." When a party of senior managers from Rolls-Royce visited Belfast to discuss the nacelles project they were not greatly impressed by the low level of activity in the aircraft factory but a visit to the nearby manufacturing facility for Seacat reassured them regarding Shorts' capability.

PERSONAL QUALITIES

· ·

What qualities did Philip Foreman bring to the very demanding role of Managing Director? His own assessment is that he was very dedicated to the task, working long hours and taking few holidays. He admits to a fascination with test work, getting test results and analysing them was always a source of great interest. But as MD he had to learn to delegate, an art of management which he found more difficult to master than others. He was a details man and always wanted to fully understand all aspects of a project; he feels that he was good at asking key, pertinent questions. He demanded the highest standards of his team but no less than he asked of himself. He was a good team player and also a motivator, "Setting the policy, welding the team together and keeping it driving forward." His personal mantra was that cost effectiveness began with sound, uncomplicated engineering design, "If the design of a product is unduly complicated no amount of effort on the shop floor will bring about manufacture at a competitive cost." Innovation and enterprise were encouraged but on the basis that technological development would be evolutionary, technical risk was managed by this step by step approach. Propositions which involved technological innovation without demonstration of their practical feasibility were treated with caution. Realism was encouraged, as well as listening to the prospective customer – with the proviso that the purchaser had to be made fully aware of the likely effect of any change of specification on costs. Common sense and uncomplicated

reasoning were advocated, "It either worked or it didn't. It was either likely to make money or not." Shorts could not afford to "bet the company" on a daring venture. It simply did not have the cash resources to gamble for high stakes. Investment was made in activities which carried a better than even chance of success. Another key to success was due prominence and value being given to each important and interlocking section of a commercially run business: design, production, sales and contracts. Key members of the Shorts team included Tom Carroll, Chief Engineer (Aircraft), Tom Johnston, Chief Aerodynamicist (Aircraft), Malcolm Wild, Head of Projects (Aircraft), Denis Tayler, Chief Test Pilot, Brian Carlin and Ken Brundle, successively the MD's Personal Assistant, Bob Manvell, General Manager (Guided Weapons), Dick Ransom, Chief Project Designer (Guided Weapons), Frank Maguiness, Chief Draughtsman (Guided Weapons) and Eric Rawson, Chief of Production (Guided Weapons). On the composites side there was George Crawford, who later rose to the position of Vice-President. Over the years the weakest link in the team had been the finance function. This was remedied by the recruitment of Roy McNulty in 1978, who took a great burden off his boss and indeed when Sir Philip Foreman retired in 1988; he was the outstanding candidate for Chief Executive Officer.

I was fortunate enough to meet with half a dozen former senior managers who spent over 200 years between them on the company payroll and who knew Sir Philip well. I asked them for their views. They replied that he was deeply respected and indeed revered, well-organised and with a lively intellect. He was described as great to work for; giving his staff support when personal or family matters arose. He encouraged individual initiative, was very affable and straightforward in his approach but did not suffer fools gladly. By nature he was highly competitive, was reluctant to take no for an answer, liked winning and wanted the people around him to have a similar attitude. He was a decisive leader and always took the final responsibility but not before consulting his Heads of Department or any others at a lower level who could provide the required input. He carefully assessed all the available information before coming to a conclusion regarding a strategic decision or the line to take at an important meeting. He was smart enough to know what he didn't know and was never afraid to seek advice. He did not stand upon rank or ceremony and was always an accessible and visible presence. In the words of one of his Directors, "He was anything but a remote voice on the other end of a telephone." At meetings, he was always fully briefed and knew what he wanted to say or what was the preferred outcome; when the right moment came he "went for the jugular". He could be vociferous in expressing his displeasure at any piece of work which did not come up to the standard he expected but equally did not hesitate in giving praise or a pat on the back when it was due. A very close but junior colleague remembers, "dancing eyes which could charm or transfix." There was never any doubt that you knew where you were with him; in the Ulster expression, "There were no back doors til him." This was appreciated and respected even when he was being a fairly hard taskmaster from time to time – such as when a bidding proposal had to be re-written at short notice or an aircraft simply had to be ready and available for the Farnborough Airshow. This was not resented, as his staff knew that he put in longer hours than any. It was all for the company's good and not for any form of personal aggrandisement and

more often that not, he was right. He knew the company and its personnel's capabilities and also what was achievable in engineering terms. He took the trouble to build up a relationship with the unions and the shop stewards; they did not always see eye to eye but again the respect was there. Though not a politician by nature or inclination, he was no innocent abroad, when he was fighting Short's corner against those who valued the company less than he did he could be formidable, especially when facing up to Government or the Civil Service. He had a deep distrust of the motives of politicians when they were making decisions which would affect the livelihood of the Short's workforce in Northern Ireland.

When thinking over this meeting with the Short's "old hands", the most apt comparison which came to my mind was with a group of ex-professional footballers gathering to reminisce over the life and character of Sir Matt Busby or Bill Shankley, or in Northern Ireland terms, Billy Bingham!

Another major consideration was the provision of a workforce with all the necessary skills; Sir Philip later commented in a conversation with Eric Waugh, "When we began (at Castlereagh in the 1950s) there were very few electronic engineers in Northern Ireland. We had to get them trained. So we built up a very capable team at Castlereagh. The engineering design team at Castlereagh was probably about a hundred strong altogether at that time. But these electronic engineers were like gold dust. And you couldn't stop them leaving. A lot left for other firms in Northern Ireland which were looking for people to do precision electronic work. They recruited from us as we were a pool of desirable labour."

RELATIONSHIPS WITH GOVERNMENT AND CIVIL SERVICE

Keeping the company busy and solvent was not assisted by the less than happy relationship with the Government in Westminster. It put a complete stranglehold on any sort of initiative or freedom of action and was in many ways a millstone around the company's neck, which had to go cap in hand for funding to the Ministry of Aviation or its successors rather than being able to avail of the normal commercial processes. The Chairman in the mid-1960s CE "Denis" Wrangham had been resolute and fearless in standing up to what he regarded as less than fair treatment from the two responsible ministers, Roy Jenkins and Anthony Wedgwood Benn. His efforts to put together a group of entrepreneurs to buy the company were faced with a negative response. In mid-1967 he was summoned to the Minister's office from the dentist's chair (possibly the lesser of two evils) to be fired – though he was given the option of resigning. From that time onwards the new Managing Director felt that he had to fight Shorts' corner against all-comers and especially Whitehall.

Fortunately the Department of Commerce at Stormont was more supportive and the Prime Minister, Terence O'Neill was positive and helpful. Sadly, as the decade wore on, the first signs of civil unrest appeared. Sir Philip remembers a poignant but prophetic moment one Sunday morning when he was flying to London from Aldergrove. Sitting alongside was Terence O'Neill, who was browsing through a large pile of the Sunday papers. He turned in his seat and said, "Phil, somebody's going to be killed here before long and it will then become a whole different ball game." O'Neill, he felt, was a good man with his heart in the right place – one of the very few politicians he felt merited such an accolade.

CE Wrangham at Shorts' Berkley square office in London with Lord Brabazon of Tara. They are looking at a photograph of the Short No2 in which Brabazon won the Daily Mail's £1000 prize awarded to the pilot of the first British Aircraft to fly a circular mile on October 30th, 1909

Terence O'Neill "A good man with his heart in the right place"
(AUTHOR'S COLLECTION)

KEEPING THE
COMPANY AFLOAT

The re-engined Skyvan, wings for the F.28, nacelles for the RB211 and missiles were keeping Shorts afloat. A new missile was being developed to add to the highly successful Seacat, Tigercat portfolio. Blowpipe was designed as a shoulder-launched, man-portable weapon. It was compact and responsive, taking only 20 seconds to warm-up and, not being

Testing Blowpipe at Helen's Bay

Blowpipe

a heat-seeker like Stinger it could take a target head-on. Some development work was carried out at Shorts' Guest House and

farm at Helen's Bay. Dummy missiles were tested by being fired into a haystack. The first shoulder firing was in 1968 and in time it would win multi-million pound orders from the British Army, the Royal Marines and overseas customers. The principal of "engineering simplicity through design innovation" is well illustrated by the guidance and control system developed for Blowpipe – the rotating nose missile concept, which is simple but highly effective. Blowpipe was the first missile built by the company which was fully assembled in Northern Ireland. This required the establishment of a secure site where the explosive warhead could be handled safely. A former Admiralty torpedo testing depot near Crossgar was selected and was supplied with the explosives by air firstly by Skyvan or SD3-30 from Glasgow to Aldergrove and from there by RAF helicopter to Crossgar.

Unfortunately a very tricky period was just around the corner. Rolls-Royce had over-extended itself with the RB211 programme and was obliged to declare bankruptcy in early 1971. Some 20% of Shorts' annual turnover was derived from engine podding, so the potential implications were severe. As Philip Foreman commented at the time, "If it had happened four years earlier, we would have been absolutely sunk." Blowpipe and Seacat orders kept the company afloat while the Government bailed out Rolls-Royce.

1971 was also a very important year from a personal point of view. One person for whom Sir Philip reserves particular praise and appreciation is wife Margaret, whom he met at Shorts. They married in 1971 and over the following years Margaret was a great support, especially when giving hospitality to potential customers. Shorts' guesthouse, Rathmoyle, near Helen's Bay (which was an idea of Rear Admiral Slattery's) was of great use in this respect as foreign visitors, fearful of "the Troubles", were reluctant to stay in Belfast city centre. It had been a gracious residence and was under the domestic control of an ex-Army steward, Mr Goodfellow, who ran a tight ship. Despite the misgiving of the Civil Service, it served the company very well for many years. The land also included a farm at one time but this was sold as the cattle broke out too many times and disturbed the neighbours.

In 1972 BBC Northern Ireland's Industrial Correspondent, Eric Waugh, commented on air in the evening news programme, *Scene Around Six*, "So far well over 70 Skyvans have been sold. It has begun to score heavily as a desert and backwoods workhorse, able to perform reliably in the roughest of areas. It has proved itself as

an outstanding performer over the rugged country of the Persian Gulf and the Middle East generally. High temperatures and high altitudes make the air very thin and difficult for flying. Skyvans are used by oil companies to fly supplies out to remote desert drilling sites, carrying water, food stores, drilling-bits and staff. Operators are advised that if an airstrip will bear the weight of a fully-loaded Land Rover doing a crash stop then the ground will hold the Skyvan. In the Sheikdom of Oman, the Sultan has eight Skyvans in service evacuating casualties and carrying supplies for the war against the rebel forces in the mountains, where they can also carry paratroops."

As for everyone in Northern Ireland daily life continued against the turbulent and often frightening background of "The Troubles". The worst period that Sir Philip now recalls was the time of the Ulster Workers' Strike in 1974. It was impossible to get into the office, work in the factory had come to a standstill and the threat of the complete breakdown of civil society was very real. Some of Shorts' customers became very restive, indeed Boeing threatened to come over and remove all its jigs and tools to Seattle. The threat of sabotage or a terrorist bomb was ever present. To add to this there was pressure from the Trades Unions and the Fair Employment Agency, which were not necessarily pulling in the same direction nor were they at all times capable of seeing the big picture – the vital importance of keeping Shorts as a going concern to the deeply wounded Northern Ireland economy. The local media was generally supportive, always bearing in mind that they were by nature conditioned to look for the sensational angle on a story.

OFFERS AND OPPORTUNITIES

1974 brought the offer of another job. Iver Hoppe was requested to resign from his position as managing Director of Harland & Wolff. The Chairman approached Philip Foreman and asked him if he would be interested in taking over. Despite his previous experience working for the Admiralty he decided that he didn't know enough about ships and (thankfully for Shorts) stayed where he was.

Another interesting proposition at about this period came from the Secretary of State for Northern Ireland's office. The Minister of State rang Philip Foreman one day and told him confidentially that Rolls-Royce was pulling out of its factory in Dundonald. They met at Stormont, were he was asked if Shorts could take it over and so avoid job losses. Philip Foreman replied that he could if the Minister would tell him what he would like to manufacture there. This is a good example he feels of ministerial wishful thinking and the expectation that an airy disregard of practicalities could solve a political problem. It is also of interest to note at this point that Shorts employed some 6000 people at this time and the annual turnover was some £40 million.

THE SD3-30

Two highly successful in-house designs were derived from the Skyvan, the first of which was the 30 seat SD3-30. The wingspan as compared to the Skyvan was increased by some 15%, the fuselage was stretched, a retractable undercarriage was fitted, the powerplant was changed to Pratt & Whitney PT6s and the standard of passenger comfort was greatly enhanced. This was not all, as the structure of the aircraft was completely reassessed and the design was made compatible with the rules applicable to light transport aircraft rather than light aircraft. Whereas the Skyvan was a flying truck best suited to hauling people and outsized loads into remote areas with short and undeveloped airstrips, the SD3-30 was a mini airliner designed to appeal to discerning passengers used to the comforts normal on the medium or long haul flights which would connect with the routes plied by the SD3-30. The first flight was made by G-BSBH on August 22, 1974, in time for

Shorts 330 N51DD of Command Airways

Shorts 330 G-BDBS, the pre-production prototype, now part of the Ulster Aviation Society's collection

the Farnborough Air Show (at which the sale of the 100th Skyvan was also announced).

Sir Philip remembers a discussion between the Chief Engineer, Tom Carroll, a somewhat blunt-spoken Englishman, who had wartime experience of baling out of an aeroplane, and the Airworthiness Requirements Board (ARB) about the size of the pilots' roof mounted escape hatches. Tom settled the discussion by remarking that, "It's remarkable how small a hole you can get through when the aircraft is on fire and the flames are licking at your backside!"

The company's sales brochure, which changed the official designation to Shorts 330, described the aircraft's attributes, "This 30-seat, luxurious, highly economic aircraft introduces completely new standards to the world's commuter passengers and airlines. It is the first wide-body design developed specifically for short-haul operation. and incorporates a range of passenger-appeal features unique in its class - walk-about headroom, air-conditioning, large windows, luxury seating, overhead lockers, galley and toilet facilities and in-flight cabin service. Complementing its big jet comfort, the 330's PT6A-45R turboprop engines, driving five-bladed Hartzell propellers, make it one of the world's quietest airliners. It is the logical growth vehicle to replace Metro, Twin Otter, Beech 99 and similar aircraft on developing networks." It was aimed specifically at short-range regional and commuter traffic in the USA, following a decision by the US CAB to permit commuter and air taxi operators to use aircraft carrying up to 30 passengers. This was something of a triumph for Shorts, a relatively small UK-based company influencing the decision

makers in Washington, "Our first major marketing task was to persuade the CAB that we had a viable proposal for a 30-seat commuter aircraft and that we were prepared to put it into production if the operating rules were amended."

A 330 for Golden West Airlines

The first airlines to put the 330 into service in North America were Command Airways of New York, N51DD, and Time Air of Alberta, Canada, C-GTAS, in the second half of 1976; the first revenue service being on August 24, between Lethbridge, Calgary and Edmonton, Alberta. Sir Philip later commented on the success of the 330, "fortunately no other manufacturer followed our lead and for some years we had this market niche entirely to ourselves." One of the problems which had to be contended was an - at times - adverse sterling/dollar exchange rate which greatly affected profitability on sales. In service the 330 proved to be reliable and cost-effective. Sales in the USA were helped by the "Deregulation" policy of 1978 which served to stimulate wide demand for increased commuter services by removing government control from commercial aviation and exposing the passenger airline industry to market forces.

US Army National Guard C-23B in flight

US Army C-23Bs

The first C-23A for the USAF under construction

A total of 179 330s/Sherpas were produced, the final one being the last of 16 enhanced performance Sherpa C-23B light freighters for the US Army Air National Guard in August 1992. At the handover of the final aircraft, K16, in August 1992, the Vice-President Operations, Ken Brundle said, "This line of historic aircraft covers thirty years of development, production and support, during which time 460 aircraft were delivered worldwide, with the vast majority still in extensive use today."

Previously, 18 C-23A Sherpas had been supplied to the 10th Military Airlift Squadron of the US Air Force and had given excellent service as part of the European Distribution System of spares support for combat aircraft, winning numerous awards and with the Company consistently being graded as outstanding

C-23A Roll-Out August 8, 1984

with Contractor Logistics Support. The C-23A (G-BLLJ/30512) made its maiden flight on August 6, 1984. The first two aircraft were handed over to the USAF in November 1984 just eight months after the announcement of the contract award. The Sherpa was fitted with a full length rear ramp door which permitted the handling of the variety of loads required, ranging from LD3 containers up to the TF30 engine with afterburner. 28 more C-23B+ aircraft were supplied to the US Army ANG - converted from ex-civil Short 360s. In recent years these aircraft have given very valuable service in Iraq, but that is a story for another day (see page 76-77 for some recent photographs).

The US Army ordered four 330s for use at the Kwajalein Missile Range in the Marshall Islands

SUCCESS IN THE USA

Selling the Sherpa in the USA was the moment that gave Sir Philip one of the greatest pleasures in his career. It was the first time that the US Armed Forces had bought a British aircraft for 40 years. He recalls that the story began with a meeting at the Pentagon with a group of US Air Force generals in June 1982. Thereafter it was quite a battle over a period of 18 months; strong support was given by the Irish Government, while by contrast, the Irish National Caucus in Washington was a considerable nuisance. The specification was drawn up by General Harbour of the USAF. He wanted a small freighter to set up a Federal Express type operation in Europe for logistic support, to keep all the main air bases supplied with spares. The Skyvan and SD3-30 had been operating in the USA and Canada for quite some time but to make a real impact in the market with subsequent types really needed input from someone with a deep understanding of the US market. Fred Austin, who was an ex-TWA Senior Captain and also had been a pilot with Short's customer Golden West Airlines, set up an office in Los Angeles and recruited a Washington-based lobbyist, John O'Malley. He knew everyone who was anyone "up the Hill" and how the labyrinthine procedures of Congress worked. The deal would never have been made without these two men. Another who made a considerable contribution was the MD's then Personal Assistant, Ken Brundle. He put together the huge volume of paperwork demanded by the US authorities – the company response to the Request for Proposal which stood several feet

Fred Austin

The C-23A documentation

high, comprised 27 volumes and 10,000 pages – involving six months intensive work. At the end of the competitive tendering process only two types remained the Sherpa and its Spanish rival, the CASA 212. When the Sherpa won it was the main story on the evening 9 o'clock national news - a good news story from Northern Ireland, which was not a common occurrence over a period of far too many years. Ken Brundle recalls that some time later he celebrated with Sir Philip by sharing a bottle of port sitting on the steps of their hotel near Zweibrucken Air Base in Germany, when the 10th Military Airlift Squadron USAF accepted its C-23As and when Sir Philip was enrolled as an Honorary Member of the Squadron.

10th MAS Certificate
(FOREMAN FAMILY COLLECTION)

THE SHED

A 360 on a test flight over Shorts

The second major derivative, the Shorts 360 (or Shed as it was affectionately known by its pilots) had a lengthened fuselage which could accommodate 36 passengers and a single tailfin rather than the twin fins of the Skyvan and 330. It also incorporated a three foot fuselage plug ahead of the wing and uprated engines. These major changes assisted in reducing drag, giving a higher cruising speed and permitted an increased payload. The bottom line for the airline – seat mile costs – was reduced by 15%, with the result that the aircraft could make money at load factors below 40%. Toilet and galley facilities were improved and the baggage volume was significantly greater. The overall design philosophy was, "We will only

The Loganair Shorts 360 G-BMAR takes off from the beach at Barra, which serves as the airport for this Hebridean Island

change those systems and components which are directly affected by the airframe stretch, the engines or the tail unit or which from 330 experience have unacceptably high ownership costs arising from high replacement or overhaul costs."

The launching of the aircraft was revealed at press conferences in London and Washington DC on July 10, 1980. These unique "simultaneous" gatherings were made possible due to the five hour time difference which allowed Philip Foreman and the Executive Director (Aircraft), Alex Roberts, to fly between the two capital cities by British Airways Concorde. The MD commented, "I believe that we have demonstrated our commitment to serving the needs of the world's short-haul airlines with the 330 which has carried nearly four million passengers to date and I am absolutely sure that now we are out ahead in a niche of our own with the aircraft. We must retain

this leadership and develop the family of aircraft which we have to offer. The 360 will ensure that we can satisfy the requirements of those larger commuter airlines who need more than 30 seats but who can't survive operating the much larger turbo-prop types, particularly in an age of rocketing fuel costs, high interest rates and rapidly increasing first unit costs of those much larger aircraft."

The prototype, G-ROOM first flew on June 1, 1981, this time to meet a Paris Air Show deadline only three days later. Service entry came 18 months afterwards with N360SA being delivered to Suburban Airlines of Reading, Pennsylvania on November 11, 1982. It was put into service on the Company's 700 miles eight-city commuter route network on December 1. By 1983 Philip Foreman could claim that with 150 Skyvans sold, 112 330s ordered and promising prospects for the 360, "Over a

G-ROOM the prototype Shorts 360

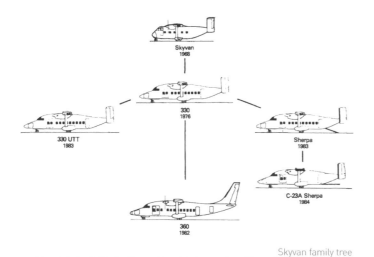

Skyvan family tree

period of 15 years we have expanded our small civil aircraft business and have grown from virtually zero sales turnover to some £40 million per annum. In so doing we have moved from

being virtually unknown to having been referred to as "the Boeing of the commuter business.""

In 1984 there were 150 Skyvans operating worldwide with 46 operators in 32 countries in a remarkable variety of roles – maritime patrol in Singapore and Japan; passenger services in Norway, Malaysia, Greece and the Maldives; oil drilling support operations in Indonesia, South America and the Middle East; highway patrol in Thailand; mail deliveries in Venezuela; paratroop training in Austria; police duties in Lesotho and Malawi; aerial prospecting in Canada; welfare work in Mexico; mid-air retrieval of rocket-borne experiments in the USA; support duties for defence forces in Oman, Nepal, Botswana, Argentina, Guyana and Panama – plus a miscellany of other roles.

In 1985 the 360 Advanced with uprated and more fuel-efficient

Shorts 360 for Philippine Airlines under construction

Jersey European flew 360s on services from Belfast Harbour Airport

David Kennedy of Aer Lingus and Sir Philip Foreman at the official handover of a 330 to the airline on April 11th, 1983

Shorts 330 and 360 seen in formation preparing for Farnborough 1982

engines entered production. The final 360 variant was the 300 Series of 1987, which incorporated a number of refinements, including six-bladed Hartzell propellers, which significantly reduced noise. The 360 proved to be a reliable and popular design which gave airlines the ability to develop routes with much less financial risk than would have been the case with more sophisticated and expensive aircraft. The break-even load factor was as low as 39% (14 seats filled). The trouble free systems and easy maintenance permitted rapid turn-arounds and a dispatch reliability figure which routinely recorded 99%. It was also well-liked by the pilots who flew the aircraft, winning the ultimate accolade, "A real pilot's aeroplane." The Chief Executive of Aer Lingus, David Kennedy, said of the 360, "It is the best aircraft in the world for the kind of routes and services we are planning." When the first 330 was delivered to Aer Lingus in 1983 he remarked that it was a particular pleasure that this acquisition to the fleet was an Irish aircraft built in Belfast.

The 360 was also described as, "A benchmark commuter airliner on which many airlines cut their teeth." Production ceased in 1991 with the last of the line being delivered to Rheinland Air Services after 164 examples. A survey of regional aircraft in 1993 gave the 360 this testimonial, "For regional airlines requiring a tough, unpressurised, 36-seater with a modest range, the Shorts 360 is probably an ideal choice."

The last 360 to be built along with many of those who helped build 360s over the years

A VISIT TO ROMANIA

A proposal was made at one stage to produce the 360 under licence in Romania (a similar scheme had been a reasonable success involving the BAC 1-11 short haul airliner and the Romanian company Rombac). Sir Philip remembers flying to Bucharest with a colleague to discuss this idea. At that time Romania was under the repressive regime of Nicolae Ceausecsu, so a full security briefing was given by MI6 in advance of departure. The men from Shorts were told to be very careful not to discuss sensitive matters in their hotel rooms or next to a pillar in the restaurant; the best option was to take a walk in the park. The flight from Belfast in the company HS125 was broken by a meeting in London to discuss Blowpipe matters. Half way between London and Bucharest Sir Philip remembered that he had some rather sensitive papers relating to the missile in his briefcase. Bearing in mind the gravity of the

A Shorts 360 of Capital Airlines takes off from Sydenham

spooks' advice, what should he do – turn back, say nothing and hope for the best or eat the documents? Instead he had a word with the pilot and requested his permission to have a little fire on board. The papers were duly incinerated and flushed away.

The hotel in Bucharest was something of a revelation, being very gloomy in the lobby but full of high class hookers in the bar on the 21st floor. They took the advice about chatting over business matters in the park, though in their business suits they felt a little conspicuous amongst the fur-clad locals in the snow. The negotiations were rather of the "good cop - bad cop" variety, involving bare rooms with plain wooden tables and chairs on the one hand and sumptuous, specially opened restaurants on the other. The departure from Bucharest seemed a bit cloak and dagger too, with a bus trip to a very remote stand and a long wait for departure clearance while watching a gang of men dig a sinister looking trench nearby. In the end nothing came of the scheme and the 360 was never built behind the Iron Curtain.

The 330 and 360 were reliable, simple to operate and maintain, were highly cost-effective and were well-loved and respected by aircrew, engineers, airline executives and passengers alike. Sir Philip's view of the aircraft may be appreciated by knowing that his car registration was FLY 360.

The basic square fuselage section of the Skyvan was retained for the two types developed from it, as was the method of fabrication, using a bonded metal structure and also the braced, high aspect ratio wing. This evolutionary family approach enabled Shorts to make full use of its investment in jigs, tools and fixtures, as well as minimising the inventory required

through the use of common parts. Most importantly from the fiscal point of view, it enabled the variants to be launched without the enormous front end funding required by brand new designs and the technical risks associated with beyond state-of-the-art technology. These benefits were passed on to the customer in the form of lower first cost of the aircraft, which in turn was reflected by lower fare levels to the passenger, with consequent market stimulation and increased sales. It can be argued with a considerable degree of justification that the Shorts family of commuter aircraft transformed short range air travel and allowed many hitherto economically unviable routes to be exploited and developed.

AEROSTRUCTURES
FLOURISHES

The aerostructures business continued to prosper. A good relationship had been established with Lockheed as the RB211 powered that company's L-1011 Tristar airliner, the wings for

Ailerons for the Tristar

which were made by Avco in Nashville. One morning, Charlie Ames, the CEO in Nashville telephoned his opposite number in Belfast and asked if Shorts would like some work making components for the Tristar – ailerons, spoilers, wing tips, undercarriage doors. He added that he never made a deal without shaking hands on it. Philip Foreman was on a flight to Nashville the next day. This, he now contends, is a good

example of the importance of personal contacts in business. The world of aerospace manufacturing was quite small in reality with everyone knowing everyone else. Therefore there was a need for companies and their senior staff to be respected and accepted within this fraternity. Sir Philip was particularly good at developing productive relationships of this sort for the benefit of the company. The company chalet at Farnborough or the Paris Airshow were regular venues at which the Foreman touch could be witnessed and appreciated, as customers and potential customers were well looked after.

A contract worth £20 million was agreed with British Aerospace in 1979 to manufacture engine pods for the BAe 146

Nacelles for the BAe 146

Inboard edge trailing flap assemblies for the Boeing 757

Main landing gear doors for the Boeing 747

regional airliner. Another very valuable contract was made with Boeing to supply wing components for the 757, adding to work already undertaken building main undercarriage doors for the Boeing 747. Later work for Boeing would include all composite rudder assemblies for the 737-300. By 1983 Shorts had delivered 1100 engine nacelle units and had risen to the second largest manufacturer in the world of these, 203 Fokker F.28 wings, 252 flight component sets for the Tristar, 345 sets of undercarriage doors for the 747 and the first 33 sets of inner flaps for the 757, with an annual turnover of £44 million.

Later a risk-sharing partnership was agreed with Fokker on the successor to the F.28 Fellowship airliner. Shorts were to design, develop and build the advanced technology wings for the Fokker 100 – which included carbon-fibre components and which made its maiden flight from Amsterdam Schipol on November 30,

Shorts-built pods on a 747 powered by RB-211s

Fokker 100 Wing Production at Shorts. As part of a risk-sharing partnership with Fokker of Holland and Deutsche Airbus of Germany, Shorts were responsible for the design and manufacture of wings for the successful Fokker 100 jetliner.

The only Belfast currently flying with HeavyLift Cargo Airlines in Australia – RP-C8020, SH-1819, formerly XR 365 Hector, G-HLFT, seen here landing at Brisbane
(PATRICK HILL)

The first step was to make composite components for the Skyvan to gain experience. A "clean room" was set up and a senior executive from Boeing, Wally Buckley, was invited over to Belfast to inspect it. As he ran his finger along a dusty ledge and asked, "Is this really a clean room?", it was one of the worst moments of the MD's time at Shorts – he felt about two feet high. However he took the criticism on the chin, listened carefully to Boeing's' advice and in 1981 a 110-ton autoclave was installed. When EH "Tex" Bouillon, the President of the Boeing Commercial Airplane Company opened the facility on

1986 – the wings having been transported to Holland in the HeavyLift Cargo Airlines Belfast G-HLFT, the first of many such trips. This was a very successful partnership until, in the mid-1990s, Fokker ran into financial difficulties and ceased operations shortly afterwards. In all Shorts built the wings for 241 F.28s, 283 Fokker 100s and 48 Fokker 70s. Fokker in turn produced the outer wings for the Shorts 330 and 360.

As part of its aerostructures business Shorts gained an enviable reputation in the field of the manufacture of composites. Philip Foreman had visited Boeing in Seattle, had been impressed by the work undertaken there and had come to the opinion that this was suitable work for Shorts, which already had manufactured some glass fibre items. He was convinced by what he had seen that carbon fibre was the way ahead and that rivets were old hat.

The 110 ton autoclave

June 11, Philip Foreman took great pleasure in hearing him pronounce himself highly impressed with what Shorts had achieved. The autoclave, which was the largest of its kind in Europe at that time, was used for the adhesive bonding of metal and carbon fibre aircraft components. The company went on from strength to strength and became one of the leaders in this field of manufacture. A manufacturing centre for components was opened in Dunmurry in the old DeLorean factory. Shorts also invested in high technology equipment – computer design systems and direct electronic links with Boeing in Seattle.

It is also of interest to note at this stage the Lear Fan project. The aircraft was the final brainchild of Bill Lear, of Learjet fame. It was a revolutionary concept, a fuel efficient, high-speed, twin engine with a single pusher propeller, 8-seat executive aircraft, made almost entirely from carbon composite material. Rather optimistically, over 1000 jobs in Northern Ireland were projected by 1984, with the assembly being based at Aldergrove. Delays in the certification of the prototype in the USA, due to technical difficulties, caused financial problems, which proved insurmountable. The plan collapsed before any local assembly or flying was achieved. All was not lost, however, as the factory and machinery in Newtownabbey was taken over by Shorts a few years later as the site for its development as a world leader in the manufactures of advanced aerospace composite structures. Sir Philip wonders to this day how the Department of Commerce in Northern Ireland could be prepared to lose several million pounds on the Lear Fan project against all the advice that it had been given that the concept was fundamentally flawed and would never receive a Certificate of Airworthiness. At least the similarly expensive DeLorean scheme did produce several hundred cars and substantial employment in West Belfast.

A programme which looked to be very promising when it was announced in 1984 was the signing of a Memorandum of Agreement between Shorts and United Technologies' Sikorsky Aircraft to submit the Sikorsky S.70A Black Hawk as a candidate to meet the MOD's Air Staff Target 404 for 75 to 125 medium-lift support helicopters to replace the RAF's Wessex and Puma fleets. Shorts would have handled the production of major components and composite parts, final assembly, flight test, delivery, modifications and post-design services. Sir Philip commented at the time, "It will further broaden the Company's industrial base and increase our proportion of military work. Additionally the technology exchange agreement under the terms of the MOA is especially significant and offers Shorts the possibility of entering entirely new fields of manufacturing technology." Sadly it was not to be, the RAF never received a helicopter under AST 404, the Wessex soldiered on until 2003 and the Puma is in service to this day.

The only Skyvans currently on the UK Register are G-BEOL and G-PIGY of
Invicta Aviation
(XAVIER POU BUSSO)

OTHER ACTIVITIES

To complete the picture, the company was also involved in flying services activities, including the provision of maintenance and operational services for military and civil organisations. Aircraft target drones were maintained and operated for the Ministry of Defence in the UK and at the Woomera range in Australia. The company also produced: the Stiletto high altitude drone, capable of exceeding Mach 2,

Skeet military aircraft target

Stiletto high-altitude drone

which was a variant of the Beech AQM-37A substantially re-engineered to meet British requirements and the MATS-B and Skeet military targets for the British Army which were designed and manufactured by the Missile Systems Division to provide a low-cost, highly manoeuvrable drone for use in practice firings of close-range missiles and guns. Shorts also designed and manufactured the Shorland range of robust, low-cost, armoured internal security vehicles – patrol cars, personnel carriers, anti-

hijack vehicles and other specialised units, all based on a strengthened version of the 109 inch Land Rover chassis. In production over three decades, the Shorlands established themselves as the best selling vehicles of their kind on the international market, seeing service in more than 40 countries.

Shorland Armoured Patrol Car

A pair of Shorland Armoured Vehicles

THE FALKLANDS WAR

A spectacular Seacat launch

During the Falklands War in 1982, Shorts products were used by both sides; Seacat by the Royal Navy and the Argentine Navy, Tigercat by Argentine Army and Blowpipe by the Royal Marines, the British Army and the Argentine Army. The company was also kept busy during the conflict, as Sir Philip remembers, the Ministry of Defence asked for top priority assistance to develop jamming countermeasures which would incapacitate the enemy's Shorts-made guidance systems. The missiles on both sides showed their utility in combat but gave the company much food for thought with regard to the development of more advanced systems. In an official statement in August 1982 the Ministry of Defence praised the effectiveness of Shorts' missiles and thanked the workforce,

"The quality of their workmanship made no small contribution to the overall success of the campaign."

A drawing of an Argentine Coastguard Skyvan
(CA GARCIA)

As regards aeroplanes, two Argentine Coast Guard Short Skyvans, PA50 and PA54, which were used for communications duties, were destroyed on the ground; while on the British side, Belfast freighters were chartered from HeavyLift to deliver vitally needed stores to Ascension Island, making something of a mockery of the decision to remove these aircraft from the RAF's inventory in 1976. HeavyLift bought five Belfasts of which up to three were in use at any one time following civil certification in 1980.

Belfast with Sea King, Harrier and Nimrod at Ascension
(BOB SHACKLETON)

COMPANY CHAIRMAN

The Company Chairman in 1983

In 1983 the recently knighted Sir Philip was asked to go and see the Secretary of State, Jim Prior, at Hillsborough Castle. They had always got on well together so he was not unduly surprised when Prior asked if following the impending retirement of the Chairman, Sir George Leitch, he would take on this extra responsibility in addition to his current brief until his retirement in five years time. Sir Philip readily agreed and was asked to sort out the details with the Head of the Northern Ireland Civil Service, Sir Kenneth Bloomfield. At the subsequent meeting Sir Philip made clear that he wanted no additional remuneration – all he asked for was to run his own ship without undue interference from the Civil Service. The Secretary of State paid tribute in the *Belfast Telegraph* to the outgoing Chairman, Sir George Leitch, "He has guided the company through a difficult period in its history. Under his leadership the company has achieved a great deal of business growth, particularly with the development of new products and business opportunities." of Sir Philip he went on to add, "He faces a considerable challenge but has established a leading position in the aircraft industry and I am grateful to him for accepting this additional responsibility for leading the company to commercial success and profitability."

Of the knighthood, a colleague remarked that it was typical of the man that the next day in the canteen, his first words were, "You know, I'm still just Phil to all of you."

A VIEW FROM CASTLE BUILDINGS

Sir Kenneth Bloomfield later wrote of his relationship with Shorts and, in particular, Sir Philip, "The combination at the top of the company, Sir George Leitch as chairman and Sir Philip Foreman as managing director was a strong one. The crucial decisions for this company to be taken in government were about levels of production and development of new aircraft. The development phase of even a very modest aeroplane was becoming hideously expensive and the return (if any) would be available only over a long period as serial production benefited from the learning curve. In my new job, I had soon become conscious of how difficult it was proving, after so many years of violence and instability, to attract new inward investment to Northern Ireland and how high were the risks in some of the newer projects. Here, at Short Brothers, we had a well-established corporate player in Northern Ireland, providing the biggest number of manufacturing jobs in the state, offering exceptional training to its young workforce and representing a high level of technological achievement. My consistent line, therefore, was to be constructively critical but fundamentally supportive. I fear the company's management – and Sir Philip Foreman, in particular – may at times have been more conscious of the first than the second characteristic. It was necessary to ask awkward questions, to demand reliable answers, to seek informative performance monitoring information, to insist on frankness about plans, performance and outlook. Sir Philip did not take easily to these constraints and our routine exchanges sometimes took on a degree of edge as consequence. I had a great deal more sympathy for him that he supposed. I do not myself like to drive or be driven from the back seat. Industrial managements with continuity are often frustrated by the regular changes in the official teams facing them – like having to educate one's own inquisitor."

Skyvan flight deck - whose hands were on the control column, Shorts, Government or Civil Service?

BELFAST CITY AIRPORT

Another interesting development came in 1983. In January, the Company's Senior Air Traffic Controller, Des Kernaghan was asked to report to Shorts' Sales Director, Alec Roberts. As a result of this interview, he was appointed as the first Airport Manager. Des recalled that this new job came his way out of the blue and he started work with an under-utilised runway, a Nissen hut and a blank sheet of paper. However, he approached this rather daunting challenge with enthusiasm. He recruited Carol Laverty and Elaine Wilson as Passenger Service Agents and prepared for business.

The entrance to the airport until 2001

It opened for business as Belfast Harbour Airport (BHD), owned and managed by Shorts, on February 7, 1983. Several of the little commuter operators opted to transfer their flights from Aldergrove to the Harbour (as it was known familiarly),

Early days at Belfast Harbour Airport

Nacelles by Shorts a BAE 146 of Jersey European comes on stand in front of the old terminal at Belfast City Airport

including Loganair, Spacegrand, Manx, Avair and Genair. It was no co-incidence that a perfect opportunity was offered to market Shorts' 330 and later 360 as the most cost-effective aircraft for smaller airlines considering using the airport. In fact Sir Philip recalls talking to Sir Michael Bishop of the Airlines of Britain Group a few months before at the Farnborough Airshow and trying to sell the 330/360 to him. "Well Chief, "Sir Michael responded, "I'll tell you what, you let me use Sydenham for my commuter operations and I will buy your aircraft." He proved to be as good as his word. He was pleased with the aircraft delivered to three of the companies in his Airlines of Britain Group and stated, "This aircraft has turned many low-volume routes which had been persistent loss-makers into profit, making a favourable financial impact on regional routes throughout the group." The management and the Board of Directors of Belfast International Airport at Aldergrove gave a very much less cordial welcome to the new airport but it was there to stay.

Within a few months, in July 1983, passenger handling at BHD moved to a new terminal. As passenger numbers grew, it was constantly modified and extended. This building, which had formerly been the RAF Officers' Mess, was used until June 2001. In 1989 the name was changed from Belfast Harbour to Belfast City Airport and subsequently in May 2006 to George Best - Belfast City Airport

Three Shorts 360s are handed over to Michael Bishop in March 1984

ADVANCED MISSILES, NACELLES AND A PRESTIGIOUS APPOINTMENT

On the missiles side, Blowpipe was developed into the more deadly Javelin, which was line of sight, radio controlled and with a semi-automatic guidance system. From 1984 onwards it

Starstreak

The man-portable Javelin

was sold to a dozen armed forces in seven countries. Later would come the even more advanced Starstreak and Starburst. Sir Philip commented, in a conversation with Eric Waugh, on these advanced missiles, "The new Starstreak factory at Castlereagh was the last capital expenditure I authorised before I retired. It was…is…a superb factory and inside it the equipment and the sort of work they are doing is unbelievable. They are working to tolerances which we thought were impossible – to tenths of a thousandth of an inch on a mass production basis." In December 1986 Shorts won a £225 million contract from the Ministry of Defence for the development, initial production and supply of the Starstreak, mounted on the Alvis Stormer vehicle, together with the lightweight multiple launcher and shoulder-launched variants, all for the British Army.

In 1985, working in partnership with the US company, Rohr Industries of San Diego, a contract was won for the nacelles and other important components of the V-2500 engine for the Airbus A-320. Sir Philip was interested in buying Rohr but the government would not consider the idea.

IAE V2500 engine nose cowl for the Airbus A320

In May 1985 Sir Philip was elected as the 100th president of the Institution of Mechanical Engineers. The first president was the famed railway engineer, George Stephenson in 1847. In later years he was followed by the famed trio of locomotive designers, Sir Nigel Gresley, Sir William Stanier and OVS Bulleid. Others to have held the post included Lord Armstrong, Sir Joseph Whitworth and Sir Philip's mentor, HG Conway.

A Memorandum of Understanding was signed with Boeing in March 1986 which provided for Shorts becoming a Programme Associate on the advanced technology Boeing 7J7 150 seat, twin prop-fan airliner. It was anticipated that this would bring a

An artist's impression of the Boeing 7J7
(BOEING COMMERCIAL AIRPLANE CO.)

considerable volume of work to Belfast and was evidence of the esteem in which Shorts was held by Boeing. Sadly the project did not come to fruition and the 7J7 never took to the air.

THE TUCANO

The last type wholly built in Belfast was an adaptation of the Embraer EMB-312 design from Brazil, the Tucano. Sir Philip had meetings in Belfast and Brazil with the CEO of Embraer, Ozires Silva, whom he described as both straight talking and a

Sr Ozires Silva Chairman of Embraer with Sir Philip Foreman

nice man. A collaborative agreement was signed for Shorts to make the bid to the MOD for the supply of a basic trainer aircraft to meets the requirements of the RAF for a successor to the long-serving Jet Provost. A great struggle ensued with British Aerospace, which had reached a similar type of agreement with the Swiss company, Pilatus for its PC-9. It became in Sir Philip's words, "quite niggly and acrimonious, with much political input from the MP who represented BAe's factory at Brough." Other competitors included the Hunting Firecracker and the Australian Aircraft Consortium Wamira. Shorts won the contract because its product was assessed to be the best value for money. The first Garrett engined Tucano flew in Brazil on 14 February 1986, while the first flight of the Shorts Tucano in Belfast was on December 30, 1986 and the first production model for the RAF was ZF135, which was rolled out on January 20, 1987. At the ceremony ACM Sir

A Tucano takes-off from Sydenham

Sir Philip Foreman and ACM Sir David Harcourt Smith at the Tucano roll-out

A Kuwaiti Tucano

David Harcourt-Smith commented, "We have secured a fine aircraft for the RAF which will be effective, safe and economical to run and will ensure the continued training of military pilots to the highest standards of the Service." The

Secretary of State for Northern Ireland added, "The winning of this contract shows that Northern Ireland industry can offer quality products at the right price. Once again Shorts has demonstrated its ability to collaborate and compete successfully."

The Tucano was manufactured under licence for service with the Royal Air Force: 130, Kenya: 12 and Kuwait: 16. It was much modified from the Embraer original, with a 1150 shp Garrett TPE-331-12B engine driving a four-bladed Hartzell, fully feathering and reversing propeller, which gave higher

The Tucano production line at Shorts

In 2007 72 (R) Squadron celebrated its 90th anniversary and painted Tucano ZF 448 in a special commemorative colour scheme - flown here by Flt Lt Bobby Moore and AVO Erik Mannings

performance in terms of speed and climb rate, a stronger airframe with increased fatigue life, ventral airbrake and restyled wingtips, the fitting of Martin-Baker MB 8LC ejection seats for both crew, bird-strike proofing of the cockpit canopy to UK standards and a complete systems/radio change to ensure maximum compatibility with the BAe Hawk, to which the student pilots would proceed. It has a maximum speed of 315 mph, a maximum climb rate of 3510 ft/min and a maximum ceiling of 25,000 feet. It has been in service giving basic training at No.1 Flying Training School (now No.72(R) and No.202(R) Squadrons) since 1993. The Tucano has proven to be 70% cheaper to operate than its predecessor. It has a greater range and endurance than the Jet Provost which allows it to fly two consecutive sorties before being refuelled. According to one of the instructors at No.72(R) Squadron, its performance is comparable to that of a Hawker Hurricane Mk 1. He is in a good position to make this judgment as Squadron Leader "Shiney" Simmons has been flying with the Battle of Britain Memorial Flight for a good number of display seasons.

The last complete aircraft manufactured at Sydenham was ZF516, c/n T131, which was delivered to the RAF on January 25, 1993. E27 for Kuwait was finished in July 1991 but because of the Gulf War was not delivered until 1995.

Tucano and Jet Provost in formation

COLLABORATIVE PROGRAMMES

As further development opportunities for the 330/360 family of aircraft came to a close and a production replacement became increasingly necessary, a series of potential collaborative programmes were investigated with likely partners, who were active or interested in regional aircraft projects. In particular, in 1986/7 detailed project studies were carried out with De Havilland Canada (then owned by Boeing) to identify a new design for the 20-30 seat market. Two turbo-prop project designs were produced, a fairly conventional aircraft and a more advanced "pusher" concept, with twin-engines mounted in the tail. It was believed that this radical idea would allow for enhanced aerodynamic and propulsive efficiency. However due, in part, to management and economic problems at De Havilland, Boeing stopped all development work to concentrate on immediate production problems.

Another design study proposed a further stretch of the Skyvan, 330, 360 family – the 45 seat Shorts 450. As it would have been unpressurised, consideration turned to a more sophisticated project.

THE FJX

By this time Shorts had become rather more interested in the possibilities for a small regional jet in the 40-50 seat class. In the light of the advent of a new range of efficient turbo-fan engines, the project was rapidly developed and was revealed, complete with a full-scale mock-up of the cabin section, at the Farnborough Air Show in 1988. This was the FJX.

An artist's impression of the FJX

Conceptually it was a superb design; technically it would still have been competitive 20 years later. It was a potential world beater but would also have represented quite a challenge to Shorts' resources. It was a very attractive looking aeroplane not unlike a small Airbus or the latest Embraer E-series in shape. The Sales and Marketing Director, Alex Roberts, commented, "The fuselage diameter now gives shoulder and aisle width

identical to the MD-80 series and is substantially larger than the proposed Canadair Challenger 601RJ." The aim was to make a firm launch decision early in 1989. Presentations were made to over 60 airlines worldwide, considerable interest being shown and a detailed technical summary/development and production cost plan was written. The government would not provide funding or support despite having poured millions into

Mrs Thatcher and Sir Philip examine with keen interest a model of the Tucano at the Farnborough Air Show

DeLorean and Lear Fan. Mrs Thatcher, whom Sir Philip respected but did not always agree with, (and who always greeted him with, "Well Foreman what have you been up to this time?") was concerned simply to sell off Shorts for the best price obtainable. It is ironic, he feels, that Short Brothers was taken over by the government in World War Two by sequestration (legalised theft?) of its entire share capital, at the instigation of Sir Stafford Cripps because it could not produce aircraft quickly enough, was not allowed to be master of its own destiny when it was a successful concern. Sir Philip still believes that this was unfair and that Shorts should have been given back its share capital and allowed to float on the Stock Market or should have been permitted to enter into a more equal alliance with Embraer in Brazil, if the political and economic circumstances allowed. In fact, if the political will had been there he would like to have privatised the company in the 1970s. If the government had backed the FJX, Sir Philip believes that Shorts could in 2007 have been in the position that Embraer is today – a world leading aircraft manufacturing company.

In Canada, Bombardier/Canadair was working on a commercial airliner developed from the Challenger business jet. When, in 1989, Shorts became part of the Bombardier Group it spelt the end of the FJX. It also heralded the end of Shorts as a manufacturer of entire aircraft. Later the missiles business was sold off to Thales and then the airport to the Spanish company, Ferrovial. Bombardier Belfast concentrated on its strengths as a manufacturer of aerostructures and component parts and also as a world leader in the field of advanced aerospace composites. It can be argued that this was inevitable and the only practical

way that the company could survive and continue to provide employment in Northern Ireland into the 21st century in such a high risk and intensely competitive business, operating at the frontiers of technology.

Cargo operator BAC Express has a fleet of five Shorts 360s including G-EXPS shown here
(AUTHOR'S COLLECTION)

CONCLUSION

By that time Sir Philip had, of course, retired (in March 1988) and so could no longer exercise any direct influence on the affairs of the company on which he had lavished so much thought and care for a period of some thirty years. Since 1967 he had been in the most senior of positions as Managing Director and subsequently also as Chairman. He had taken a company which could have gone to the wall and through hard work, perseverance, will power, technical and business acumen; it had become a world leader in several fields of aeronautical manufacture – commuter aircraft, guided missiles and aerostructures – the legacy of which survives in the manufacturing heart of Northern Ireland to this day. Shorts had made headlines throughout his twenty-one years in charge. Throughout the period he had to coax and cajole a succession of government ministers in Westminster, Stormont and Hillsborough Castle, as well as permanent officials in Belfast and London – some of whom were supportive but others were either fair weather friends or not friends at all. While it is true to say that he could not have achieved all that he did without the support of an excellent management team and of a skilled workforce, the fact is that it was Sir Philip Foreman who provided the drive and the leadership. He also enjoyed unstinting support from the Chairman and Board of Directors at all times, even though they frequently had to tackle some very difficult and controversial issues mainly arising from the knotty problem of Government ownership. He really cared about

Sir Philip Foreman's retirement party with Kingsley Morse, President of Command Airways

Sir Philip Foreman's retirement party with Kingsley Morse and Lady Foreman

Shorts, it was much more than just a job and he certainly wasn't in it for the most generous of financial rewards. It is no surprise to learn that he was referred to at times and not wholly in jest as, "the fourth Shorts brother." Michael Donne wrote of Sir Philip, "He stands alongside Oswald Short as one of the two great architects of the company's activities, together spanning 64 years of its history." This dedication and deep personal commitment is I believe the outstanding feature of his time in charge, for which he deserves to be remembered with respect and gratitude.

A C23 Sherpa of 185th Aviation Regiment, Mississippi ARNG awaits her crew for another night mission in Iraq

(US ARMY)

REFERENCES

Airplane, The Complete Aviation Encyclopaedia, Parts 54 and 180

Bloomfield, Sir Kenneth, A Tragedy of Errors The Government and Misgovernment of Northern Ireland, Liverpool University Press, 2007

Cooke, Charles A, Skyvan Survivors, Air-Britain Digest, Autumn 1997

Donne, Michael, Pioneers of the Skies, Shorts Brothers plc, Belfast 1987

Donne, Michael, Flying into the Future, Shorts Brothers plc, Belfast 1993

Foreman, Sir Philip, Repositioning a Business in a Competitive Environment, paper to the 31st National Conference of the Irish Management Institute, April 29, 1983

Foreman, Sir Philip, The Evolution of Shorts Range of Light Transport Aircraft, 18th Handley Page Memorial Lecture to the Royal Aeronautical Society, April 11, 1984

Foreman, Sir Philip, Cost effectiveness through design simplicity, Proceedings of the Institution of Mechanical Engineers, Volume 199, No 132, 1985

Foreman, Sir Philip, Speech to the Publicity Association of Northern Ireland, March 1988

Merseyside Aviation Society and Ulster Aviation Society, A History of the Short SC-7 Skyvan, 1975

Taylor, Clayton, I'll Never Forget My Shorts, Airways Magazine, April 2002.

Smith, PR, Shorts 330 and 360, Jane's Publishing Co Ltd, London 1986

Warner, Guy, From Bombay to Bombardier, Air Enthusiast, Volumes 100 and 101, 2002

Waugh, Eric, With Wings as Eagles, Thales, Belfast 2003

A C-23 Crewman of Company E, 207th Aviation Battalion, Alaska ARNG, displays the unit patch on his flightsuit
(US ARMY)

NEWSPAPERS AND MAGAZINES

Belfast Telegraph,
News Letter,
Irish News,
Irish Times,
Financial Times,
Daily Telegraph,
The Times,
Sunday News,
Flight International,
Air Pictorial,
Commuter Air Magazine,
Forbes,
Engineering News,
Shorts sales brochures,
Shorts 330 Bulletin,
Shorts Aircraft News,
Short Story,
Short Quarterly Review.

INTERVIEWS

Sir Philip and Lady Foreman,
Ken Brundle,
Brian Carlin,
George Crawford,
Paddy Crowther,
Tom Johnston,
Dick Ransom,
Malcolm Wild,
Eric Waugh.

The Foreman Family December 2007
Sir Philip and Lady Foreman, son Grahame, Serina and their twin boys Cormac and Ambrose
(PHILIP DAVIS)

GUY WARNER

Guy Warner has been a regular contributor for more than a dozen years to the Ulster Airmail, the journal of the Ulster Aviation Society of which he is also a committee member.

As well as writing for Aeroplane, Aircraft Illustrated, Air Enthusiast, Airliner World, Air Pictorial, Airways, Air International, Army Air Corps Journal, Aviation Ireland, Aviation News, Flying in Ireland, Flight Deck, Flypast, History Ireland, Northern Ireland Travel News, Spirit of the Air and 230 Squadron Association Newsletter, he has also had several books published.

He is co-author of In the Heart of the City: The History of Belfast's City Airport, 1938-1998, Flying from Malone: Belfast's First Civil Aerodrome, Belfast International Airport: Aviation at Aldergrove since 1918, Army Aviation in Ulster, The History of No 72 Squadron RAF and author of Blandford to Baghdad: The Story of No 72 Squadron's First CO, The Westland Wessex 1963-2003: 40 Years of RAF Service, Orkney By Air: A Photographic Journey Through Time, No 230 Squadron Royal Air Force: Kita Chari Jauh — We Search Far, Airships Over the North Channel and Flying from Derry – Eglinton and Naval Aviation in Northern Ireland.

Guy is married with two daughters and lives in Co Antrim.

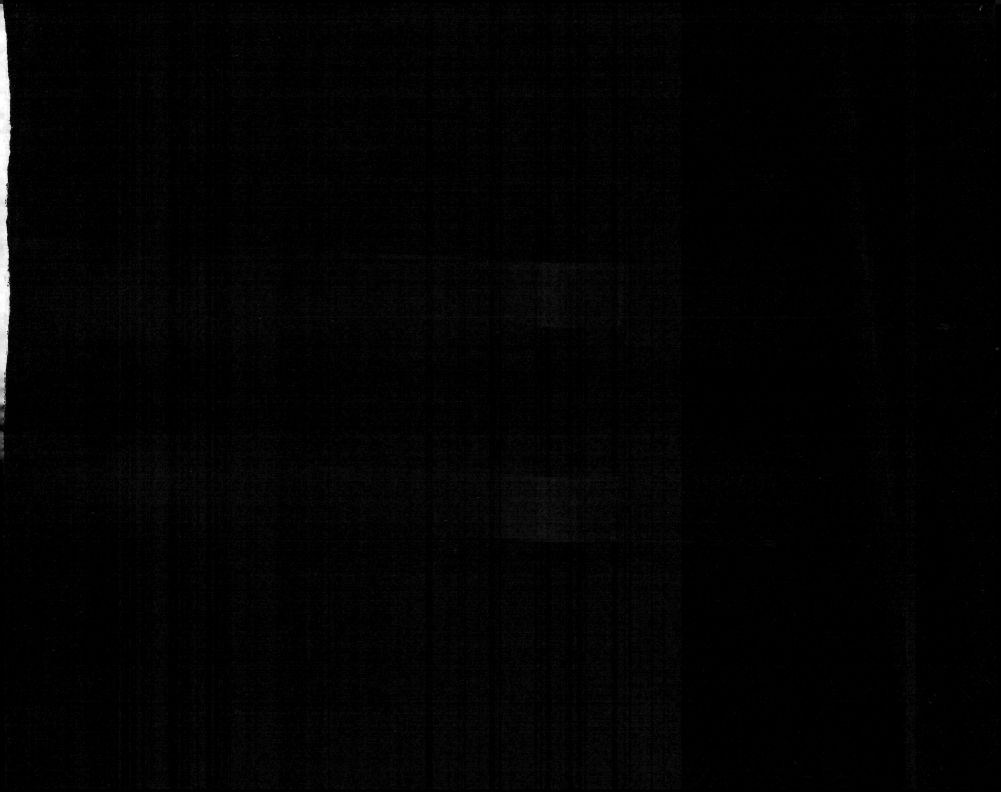